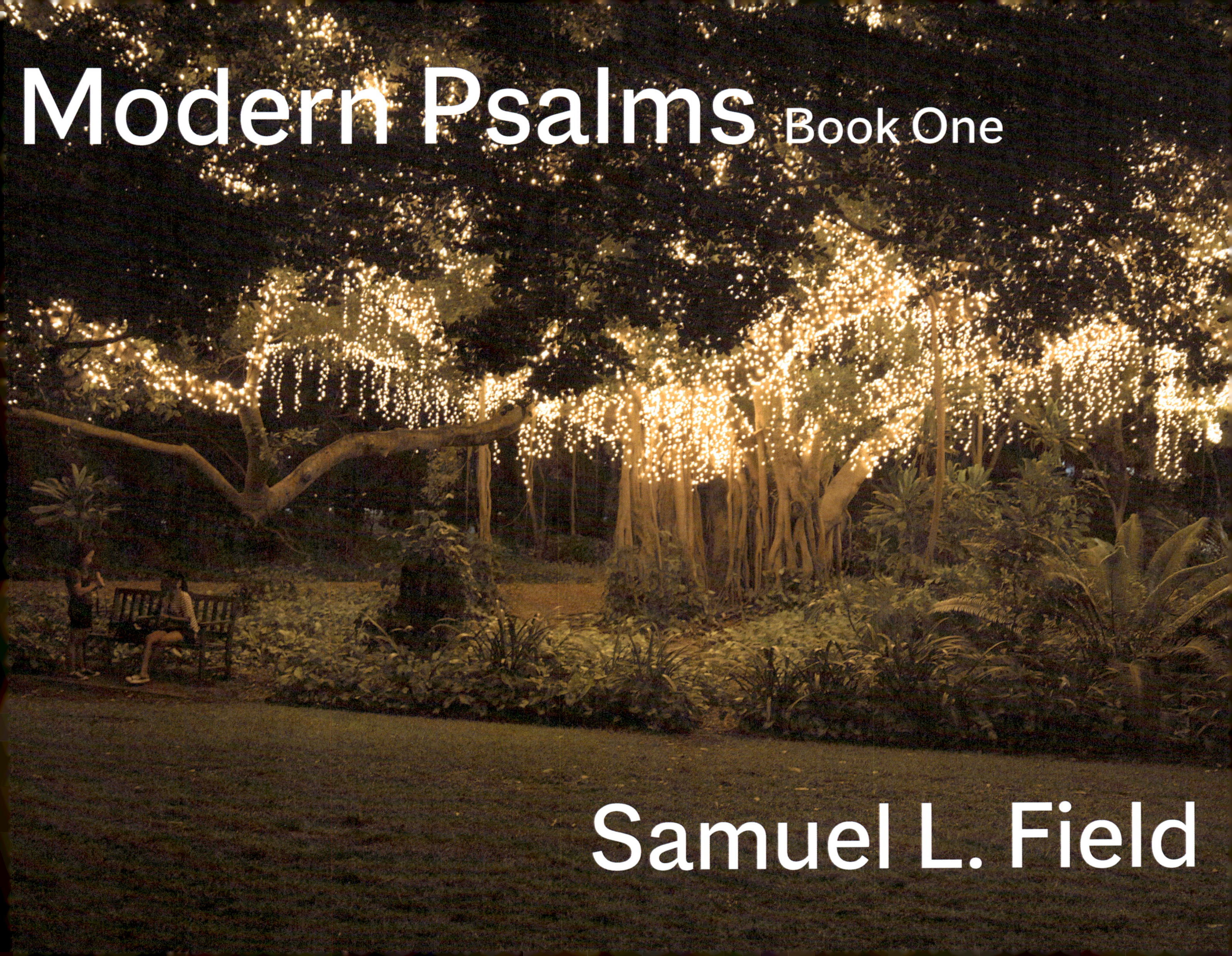
Modern Psalms Book One
Samuel L. Field

Cataloguing-in-Publication entry is available
from the National Library of Australia
http://catalogue.nla.gov.au

First Edition Published 2024 by YndFwd Creative

www.yndfwdcreative.com

www.samuelfield.com

Modern Psalms
Book One

One book a year, then in year five, not this time, not this book. It's not written for now, for a moment. It's written about and to The Eternal One. While I imperfectly pour pieces of my heart, my mind and my soul into words, layered on these pages, I hope you see Who I have seen, Who I have come to know. I hope you can see past my eyes to Who is worth more than can ever be acquired. To The Source all of life and freedom. To the One who waits for each hearts turning towards.

As the Lords prayer starts with an acknowledgment of who God is, so the first two chapters focus on who God is, His Love and His character. Then on who we are, and who we are joined to The Christ. Chapters three and four move to religion and relationship. God's religion is inherently for relationship and what He values, and is the only one to want. Choosing to focus on what He wants, and not in other directions. So I write to this clarity, to the 'eyes on Me' that He desires. Let God's religion be my only religion, it's a lighter load.

Much effort has been made in sharing from my journey to ensure these words are honest and insightful, essentially my best for The Highest. I hope what you hear when you read them, resonates to you.

Chapter 1 - Crying Holy

Crying Holy	5
Worship	7
Oh Mysterious King	8
My Source	10
My Praise	12

Chapter 2 - Eternal Love

Why?	14
Give	15
Compared	16
Why Do You Love?	18
Forgiveness	20
The Aleph & The Tav	22

Chapter 3 - Reform Me

Rivers Course	24
Dirty Water to Wine	26
Send Your Fire	28
Love's Furnace	28
Overflow This Waiting Heart	30
Validation	32
Lover	34
Wife	37
Royal Blood	38

Extras

Photo List	62-65

Chapter 4 - Just You

Universal Truth	40
Religious Roadkill	42
Carting God	44
One Body Only	45
The Grace Card	48
Sin Uses Truth	51
Truth Not A Lie	52
The Crack	55
Three Generations	56
How Did I Hurt God?	58
Our Religious Choke-holds	60

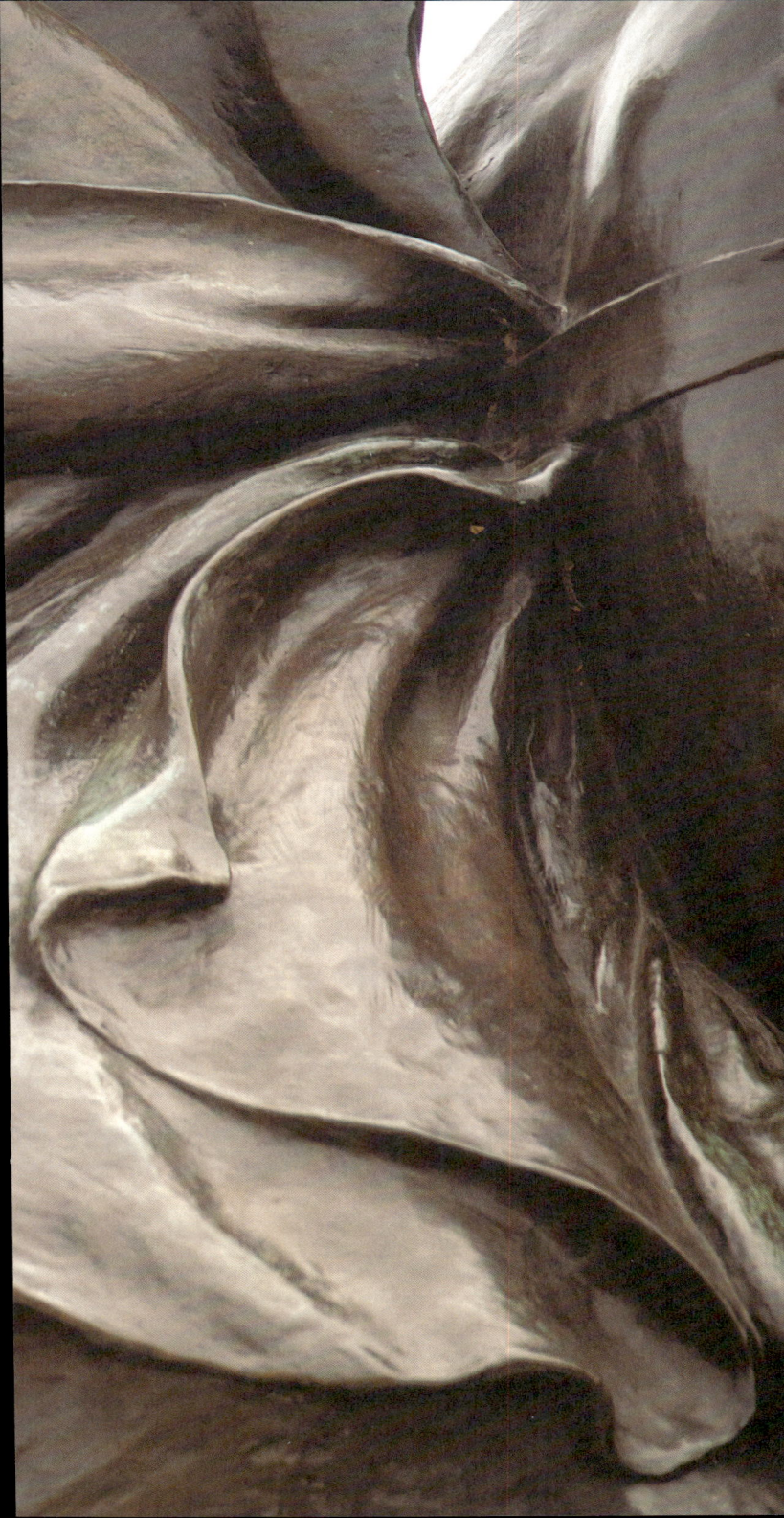

Crying Holy

Elders fall before
Divine Love enthroned
Declaring His nature and glory
Crying because they continually see
Truth again overwhelms their being
They cry what creation yearns to
They cry what only the free see

Holy, Holy, Holy
Is the Lord God
Almighty now
From before
And is to be

Holy, Holy, Holy
Is The Holy I Am
Only Giver of life
He re-gives freely
To turned hearts
Who now seek

Holy, Holy, Holy
Is He who blesses
With real truth
The hearts call
To freedom in

Holy, Holy, Holy
Is the tearer of all veils
The opener of deep ways
Calling the willing seeker
For hearts He waits

Holy, Holy, Holy
Caller, Redeemer, Lover
Beckoning a closeness
To mysteries shared

Holy, Holy, Holy
Elders keep crying
Falling before Glory
For they have sought
Been found, and seen
Deep mysteries of You
Holy, Holy, Holy

Worship

I am on the floor again
Face down in worship
As my heart lays
Before Yours

I hear Your words
On my lips, to my ears
As this will, surrenders
In Your Love's presence

You speak reality to hope
Breathing life again in me
Now raising my dreams
From their early graves

So I willfully submit
My heart binds deeper
Devoting itself to Yours
Your strength flows in

As I live in Your presence
I am lifted above this world
All the worries that seek to bind
Burdens now and past, discarding

Piecewise taking off pretense, pride
Learning to surrender to, and as I Am
Your Loving will becomes sufficiency
Your Love's will, never fails, or leaves

Oh Mysterious King

Oh Mysterious King of All
Your words frame reality
And yet, by Your breath
Life's been given to us

How You give Love
To weak such as we are
Form molded by wet dirt
Yet in this You breathed
And eternity is in me

Yet I trip on, and into
My existential angst
As this body learns
And further knows
Its many decays

Men find ways
To destroy men
This world knows
Many broad decays
So numbered days
Was another gift

Each gift has limits
Many to oft abused
We carry the Breath
In mud we remold by
Our choices each day

Yet the glory of kings
To seek meaning in layers
Embedded in Your framing

Pearls of wisdom
Adorn creations neck
Glory shown to seekers

This eternal purpose
To make kings of men
Who seek deep Truth

Existential chasms
Distances so vast
You span it all

Gifting the seeker doors new to open
I can't choose how, when or where
Yet open doors find me deeper in

Tensions within interdependence
Inalienable weaves of creation
The earth yearns to cry out

Creation waits to show praise
His goodness to be seen plain
Placed by The Mysterious King

The seeker who holds past
Their noises and comforts
Are reached from beyond

One in Three
Inseparably Unique
An unfolding in eternity

The limit of limitless
Are all moments given
By the Lord of All Time

Holy, Holy, Holy
There is only One
All Holy is of The Holy

The patient Holy
The Truth is found
When seekers are true

My heart seeks this Truth
Hidden in creations plain sight
Freedom from the eternal night

My Source

A tree raises its branches, its leaves, its life to the sun
Such vast distance, part closed in its small way
So my life, soul and my spirit, rise to the Son
Reaching towards Love who feeds me
Flowing over, of all overflowing
Folding Love, into this life
Feeding myself and
Others who pass
My shelter
And fruit

My Praise

Shattering the lies
Of false perspectives
Seeing not just reality,
Also the fabric
Woven by One
In all truth
There is by One Truth
The One is Truth
As there non-true outside
The One
The I Am

This is obscured
To a great degree
By the lies sprayed
Into views
A few look through
So that the gentle one
The counselor
The peace prince
Opened each
Piece-fully

From dimly seeing
I'm falling on my face
Crying Holy, Holy, Holy
Saying Holy is the One
Who was, is, and comes
Who holds threads of time
And weaves my story in them
And yours too
And said it is good

He dreamed of us
Conceiving our existence
As good
As pleasing to Him
              Even when I dragged my
     Fragile tapestry where it would tear
He waited for my yielding
And He waited as I handed
Over my life piece by piece
And I got peace, by peace
This deeper connection
To The I Am
To all
To The Good
In the nature of His creation
His Nature
So I cry

My praise
Holy, Holy, Holy

Why?

Oh God of Heaven
The world cannot contain You

Who am I, that I Am

Would visit upon me?

Give

I want to give glory to God
I want my life to glorify Him
I have only myself to give

Yet I am part of His glory
So I give You
Me

Compared

Oh me, a disobedient child
You say wait and I chafe
You said stay and I raced
Oh my Father thank you
My childishness is nothing
Compared to Your grace

Why Do You Love?

Why do you love my broken soul?
I have no riches to pledge
And little glory to share
My followers are few

Yet You wrap me up, gently
Blanketing my weak soul
As the cold of this world
Again saps my strength

I am sorry I kept expecting
You would stop Loving me
Loosing interest in me
If I didn't give enough

What could I give You?
You're The Giver of all I have
And yet all wouldn't be enough
All would be but a partial return

I can give all my heart, yet
Compared with Your Love
What love I have is so little
Yet My heart is Your desire

Why do You call me worthy?
I heard about the price paid
Your choosing such cost
To claim me as worthy

Yet, why me?
I could never repay You
No deal could be struck
With fair, even part-paid

I have struggled accepting such
No other Love has stood so firm
In every storm that floored me
You were always waiting for me

No other love is so strong
Where else would I turn?
No other love has stood
So with what I have, I stand

I can't give You back
Anything You didn't give me
Yet I can choose to Love You
Now, and tomorrow's tomorrow

I want to
Every storm
Every great day
Every day, You give me

Forgiveness?

Scarred hands and side pierced
You accepted our injustices
You accepted our violence
You accepted our lowest
You accepted our pain
You carry scars too
You raised above
Not just on cross
Not of perfect body
Not of angry judgment
But a higher standard of Love
Unearned injustice met, unfair Love
You met our imperfect, perfectly
You loved who, unknowingly
You loved who, knowingly
Tore Your flesh and life
Yet You did it for us
For Your Love

The Aleph And The Tav

Oh Alpha And Omega
Unchanging One
Rock of Ages
Love

Expressing Your heart and glories
Your love painted in Your giving
What beauty is in this world
What beauty is in your plan
As it was in Your garden
So it will be in heaven
Our father is walking
With man's children
Those in His image
Formed to His will
Ever companions

As slave, son and king
Formed in clay carved
A Three-folded destiny
Bisque fired in my life
With choices stained
Often through pain
Purified and keen
Glazed in blood
Of the Given
Not taken

My will suffers
To heart reformations
As selfish centers' surrender
To a Love, large enough for all

Taken by joys
Taken to Love
Taken into peace
Taken in surrender
This heart that sees
The generosity of life
Past the pains of strife
Past the entitlement lies
That I am owed a free ride

Life given twice
The depth of this gift
Undeserved both times
Because Father deems a life
Because Father loves His child

His always Will
In eternal life, shared
Temporally distorted by
Lies of not His way, by ours
That we will exist alone
In existential self gift

After Adam and Eve chose exit
It became ours now to choose
To re-enter a door held open
Till the stars are all there

Turning to Him I say
Not my will but Yours
The one linked to life
Fullness from now
Till stars pass

Rivers Course

As water in all rivers follow a cut path
Of cause my river followed a course
Till droughts brought my flow low
In dirty waters of slow flow
Do I just await its settling
It's pain in suspension

Floats in swirls around me
My life's away from new flow
Can one can live on dirty water?
Rain on the banks might bring plenty
Yet in avoiding new dirt I wallow
In stagnant waters of avoidance

From the floods of life has dirt been stirring
Taking stability of flow to see its fall
From the swirls of activities
That I am to leave behind
One event, or even
A speck at a time

Of flows there is only one source of clear life
Of separated water, that can wash away
Pains of past, holy waters of hope
Tracking from the original source
Before others dirtied it
Before I did too

Dirty Water to Wine

My dirty inner waters of life
A puddle isolated, stagnating
Pouring my old self in again
Playing with old meanings
My dirt of selfish churn
Quick release sought
Relief from old pain
Sloshing within
You cup what's
Left of me
Scooping up
Transforming me
Guiding, shaping me
Back to Your love's way.
Within this still clay vessel
Mixed in Your oils anointing
Restoration through Grace
My beginning and ending
My only rock in storms
Freedom from past
By Loving hands
My Saviour
My love

Hibiscus Infused Gin

Mandarin Infused Gin

BARREL AGED OLD FASHIONED

FREMANTLE HERALD

Send Your Fire

Dad send Your fire
The cost, I don't know
Yet my life, I give back

Set me on fire as Yours
Take this dross filled life
There is plenty to burn
The only fire be Yours

How You change me
I am learning all-ways
Take me, consume me
I want to burn for You

On Your altar of pure love
I lay my will in surrender
I know I will become
More than I was

Dad send Your Love
More Fire, more Love
Making me as I Am

Love's Furnace

Burn away my clutter
Of selfishness and pride
My destructive secret vices
Ego has climbed so high

Burn through my life
Remove what You choose
So I burn with Your passions
Desiring only what's of You

Fire my heart
In Love's furnace
Your passion to love
All my brothers and
Sisters of Your way
Then for all the lost
Stumbling in their
Seeking a home
They are yet
To know

Overflow This Waiting Heart

Let these streams of love
Overflow from Your flood
Who can contain them?

Blessed have I been
Blessed am I now
As are all who love You

Great is Your faithfulness
Great is Your mercy
Great is Your love

All my ways are Yours
Yet this is not a gift
It is truth understood

The birds are Your delight
And so the heart that
Waits on You

Validation

The designer of earth
Who dwells above
Took on our form
Took our pains
From a cradle
To a cross
For me
For all

What other validation
Could I ever need?

Lover

Oh lover of the broken
On whom You pour love
So freely, so wantonly
In such excess

Who can You be
But holiness itself
Formed Intentionality
You are loving Your creation

Wife

You gave away all
Of life's pleasures
So I can be rescued
From my selfish wants

Then I got stingy and cheap
I valued choices for self first
Over sharing everything first
With my maker, of all my days
Who values my choices for Him

I was born of earth, then grace
Redeemed in gifted flowing place
By the husband, calling from dawn
Adam. Adam. Where have you gone?
Offering even His own life, for my return

Royal Blood

Royal blood was shed for me
On a raised altar of death
Mounted on dead tree
Displayed hillside

Raised for a world to see
Shame on the God King
Victory of the father thief
Yet it was not, all it seemed

Royal blood was shed for me
Godly, Blameless and Holy
Wholly able to restore life
His own, all, and mine too

Across the bounds of time
Has royal blood spilled wide
Shattering all binds of death
Even those deservedly earned

This Royal blood cannot be owned
By any other than This Royal Line
No thief can steal Its power
No shame can lean against It

No victory can or will It be denied
Royal Blood covers my failures
Royal Blood infuses my deep
Royal Blood sets my worth

Could I sell me cheaper?
Than the royal price
He paid for me
For now I am
Royalty too

Universal Truth

This universe was born to carry us
Flowing along streams of time
Energy to matters unfolding
Assailing lightness passing

Crying Inception from
Let there be life
Carried from light
To matters developing

Global entropy
Local homogeneity
Succor to purpose
Chaos under orders

Asteroids collided
Fish in seas thriving
Land dwellers, creatures
Humans above surviving

In turns we are terming
Ourselves enlightening
Yet surrendering in truth
We transfer the light'ening

This universe was born to die
Its purpose exhausted
Its occupants gone
Eternally

Universes many or one?
Does it matter?
Could it ever?
We yet grow

Metabolizing long sought
Fairy-tailed deeper truths
Mythologized often
Into ever afters

Religious Roadkill

Lives cast aside
If they don't service the lies
This is a trope known so well
It can't be happening here?

The whitewashed tombs
Have settled among us
Their lack of integrity
Buried within

Compassion purified
Of all real care
Too pure are they to
Have the dirty stand too close

Because it is for power
And praise, and love
From other men
From women
From afar

So now these have become rules
We are clean, if we look clean
So keep it easy to tell
On our side or not
If your in, or out

Grace, Trust & Love became
Shibboleths discarded to
Upbeat and prosperous
And outwardly clean

Worship at that alter is easy
It's made of polished bricks
Raised for attention
Only our attention

I worshiped at the white tombs
Not seeing the bones inside
While I was draining of life
Yet my God, is The God
Who raises dead to life
Who orders His man
Speak to dry bones
Who calls the heart
Looking past the flesh
Where men fix their gaze
My God walked to the unclean
Calling their hearts to be His alone
Calling them to His Name, His Love

Carting God

The ark on a wooden tray
Livestock out the front
It was an effective cart
This way they carried
The God of All that is
Men walked aside it
Until Uzzah died

He merely reached
To stabilise that which
Was never meant to be
The God of the universe
Has spoken his Will thus
It was never another way
He chooses hearts for carts

We don't carry his Word
His Will, on carts of wood
Or our own corporeal forms
We leave it to the incorporated
Standing by as they claim to carry
Structurally, professional, musically
When it is our heart He calls for first

In chosen hearts He dwells
The creator, of all creation
Within people, each one
He knows by spirit
He offers to dwell there
Regardless of organisation
Their names or effectiveness

On Peter He built a church
On a failing rock He called home
On the hearts of men He dwells alone
There is only one church of the broken
Through which Love shines through
Not because He desires our power
He is that source, never a taker

Oh heart of mine
Let me not look at the cart
To do the work you call me to
Let me not stabilise what is profane
It is one church, loving within and without
As we learn to carry Your essence and truth
In the hearts we put under surrender
To You, and to Your lighter load

One Body Only

Each body part calls itself whole
As they point out differences
Doctrines, styles, leaders
Worldly successes
Weekly dollars
Numbers
Followers
Press covers
Assigning a value
Of ours, not Christ's
Are they known more,
By their love for another?
Or by their working together
Over centuries many have tried
Shuffling doctrine, merging styles
Uniting under more popular brands
Consolidating numbers, and dividing
The people of Christ, yet more groups
There can only be one head, one Christ
And He, speaks for Himself, represented
We can only choose, to follow as we are
To present to represent as we are, today

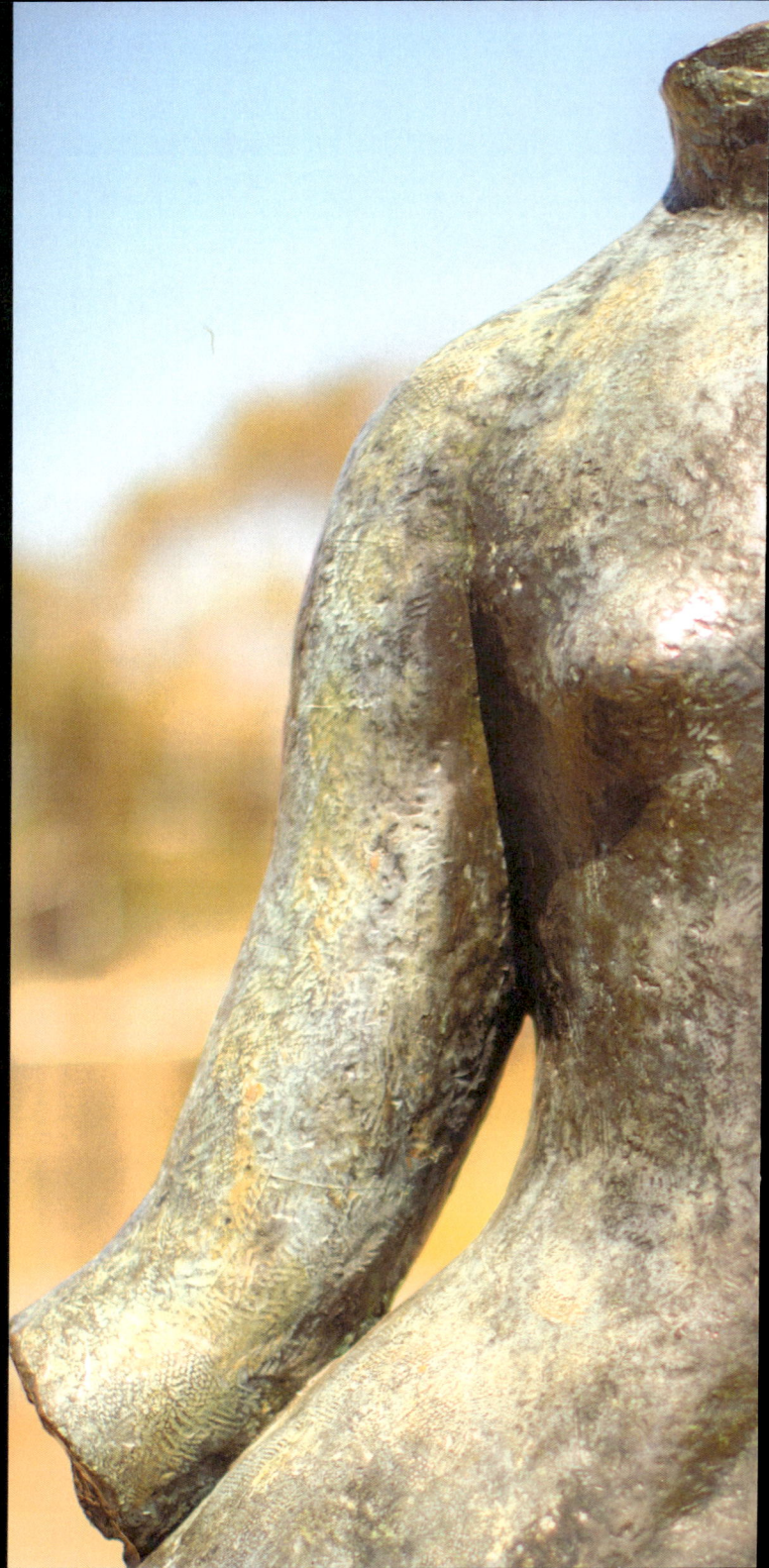

My brand is naught
There is only Christ
There is only Christ
Only Christ
Christ and
One bride
One Christ
Identity above
Either Jew or gentile
Pentecostal or Baptist
Our doctrinal purity is not
A pass to heaven or a ticket
Higher in the queue on the way
It was for all, He suffered and died
It was for all, that He made a way
It was for all of us He calls
It was for all, beyond you
It was for all, in conflict
It was for all, in denial
It was for all against
He gave all, for all
It was for the Jew
It was for Gentile
Was for your friend
Was for your enemies
It was for those arrayed
To take you down, to hurt you
Arrayed against His will, His love
He died for them too, to be His bride

Sin Uses Truth

Sin conceives in freedom
Nurturing on truth twisted
Shrinking life to deconstruction
Breaking down to be back to dust

Truth's value is proclaimed as nothing
To setup swaps of given birthrights
For promises of a future, stolen
And offered back all broken

The thieving parasitic twister of truth
Brings death premature, undignified
Life swapped and stolen gradually
Cheap chaos priced as freedom

Yet distortions powerful claims do yield
Dissolved on Truth empowered words
The death to self by insights unfolded
Freedom is re-birthing in the Word

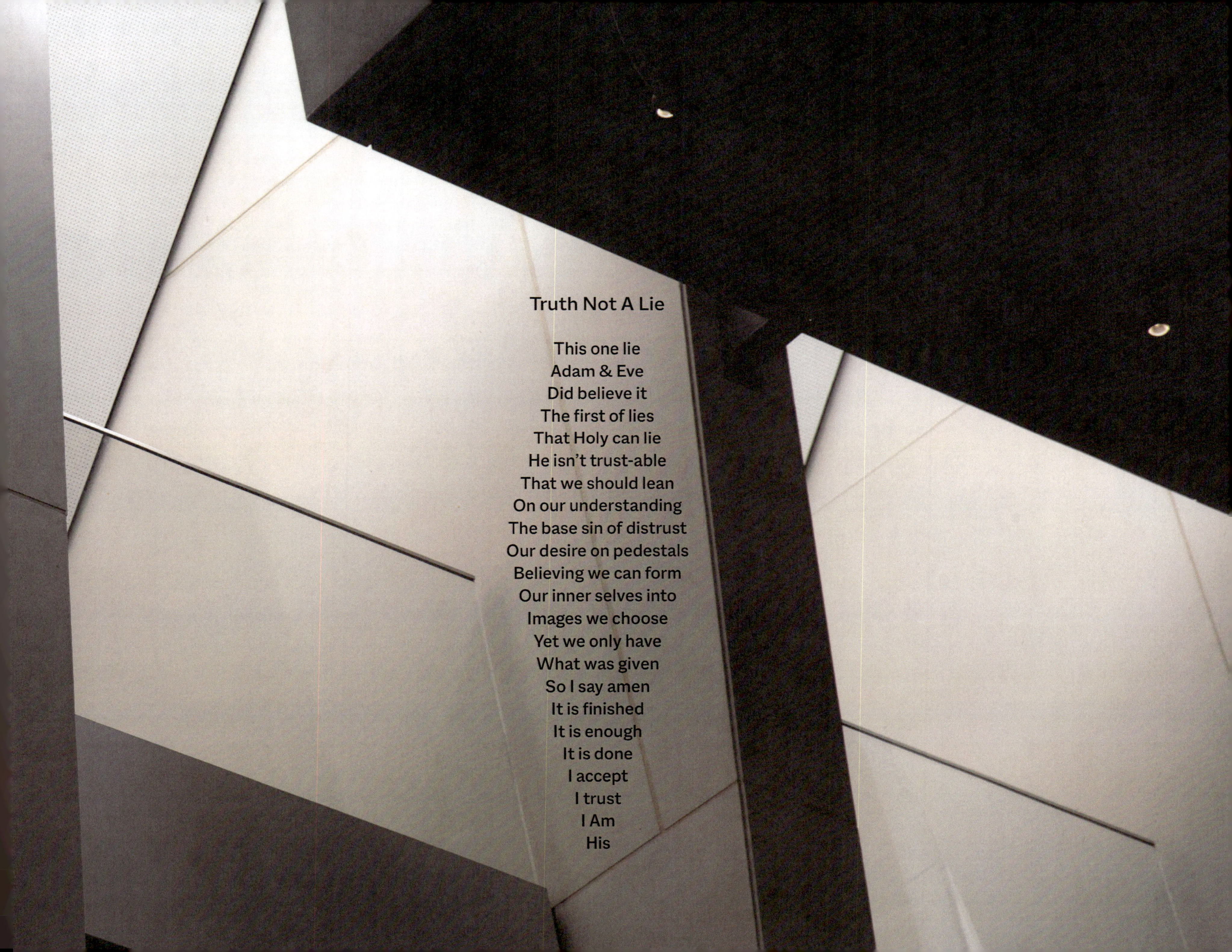

Truth Not A Lie

This one lie
Adam & Eve
Did believe it
The first of lies
That Holy can lie
He isn't trust-able
That we should lean
On our understanding
The base sin of distrust
Our desire on pedestals
Believing we can form
Our inner selves into
Images we choose
Yet we only have
What was given
So I say amen
It is finished
It is enough
It is done
I accept
I trust
I Am
His

The Crack

I considered you as The Judge
Requiring a level of perfection
Standards, I could never meet
Then as a bond holder Saviour
Requiring my good responses
Like a freedom payment plan

Getting past my small mind
Perceiving a universe created
With even me in Your mind
With my failures known
Before I earned shame
You knew me free
You paid before
I knew its need
Not to hold over
But to see my joy
You need nothing
Yet give everything

Maybe it was all the cracks
The cracks in the world I made
Mind carved images of self
My failures at perfection
By these true light got in
Seeing passed myself
Past all the stories
Religion I knew
By cracks in me
That let this light in
Beyond these stories
To the realness of You

Three Generations

Three generations of women
Arms raised in praise & surrender
An intense joy on all three faces

Although one is on stage
Another in a forward place
Something flows between
A call to intimate praise
In a family gift of grace

I can't help wonder
Seeing the grandma
She's so lost in praise
Her arms stretching
To a hearts embrace
Physically yearning
And face that says
He is wrapping her
In spirits embrace

Three generations of women
Foundations and legacies of grace
Each choose this surrender to praise

The Grace Card

Grace unearned, undeserved
Grace, so broad, so deep
Yet I'm rarely amazed

I kept choosing to do all in my own ways
Poor submitting, weak understanding
I played the grace game clever
To do what I wanted to
In my old life pride

I stumbled those roads to
Rule based sanctification
All while holding that ace
Your bloodied Grace card
Back-pocketed from salvation

How Did I Hurt God?

Why did I think it was my sin
That brought God more pain?
When it was this sin He bore
For our distance to go away

The One who dreamed of me
Who desired for my being to be
Who opens the existence door
Yet wants my turning to Him

Paying the life price
So reunification can be
He walks the earth to me
And hearts calling out to Him

Its not my sin that
Brings God the most pain
It's the loss He feels when in
Selfishness I close my heart to Him

Religious Choke-holds

My deep hearts home
So gentle to this soul
You wrap me in peace
Teaching me to reject
Man's selfish religion
And trust, You first

Oh dead religion of men
You promised me so much
From quick relief of pains to
All the riches this world offers
If I flay God gifted freedoms
You offer personal power
Yet demand too much

Man's religion
Covers not
Not all of me
Not with love
Nor with grace
Only in demands

Wounded reminders of
My incomplete failures

The law on sign posts
Measure of the Holy heights
The insurmountability of Holy
Who ascends this mountain
Unless lifted on Holy grace
From The Only Holy One

My surrender to grace
Is a beautiful art twisted
In man's slithering religion
Calling me a slave to failure
Not child of the Most High King
Seeing me as the dust I come from
The laws order was to first birth
The mechanics of a dust world
Its surrender is of self desire
And I continue to workout
This birthing of freedoms
So vast it's not grasped
Given of the God of All
Who called me out
Of choke-holds
To be as He Is

Photographs

St Paul's Cathedral and London City, from the Tate Modern, London, England

The Three Tuns, Chepstow Wales

Art Gallery of Western Australia

St Mary sub Castro, Dover Castle, Kent, England

Miss Chat's, Fremantle, Western Australia

Brisbane, Queensland, Australia

Gloucester Cathedral, Gloucester, England

Portsmouth, England

Forest Station, Western Australia

South Dock, Canary Wharf, London, England

St Anne's Cathedral, Belfast, Northern Ireland

Gloucester Cathedral, Gloucester, England

The Paddock, Wandering, Western Australia

Imperial War Museum, London, England

Dungarvan Castle, Co. Waterford, Ireland

Plantation, Gingin, Western Australia

St Paul's Cathedral, London, England

Lismore Castle, Co. Waterford, Ireland

Edinburgh Castle, Edinburgh, Scotland

David Livingstone's First Church Building, Livingstone, Zambia

Canals, Camden Town, London, England

St Curig's Church, Llangurig, Llanidloes, Wales

Peterborough Cathedral, Peterborough, England

Canterbury Cathedral Canterbury, England

Cuty Sark, Greenwich, England

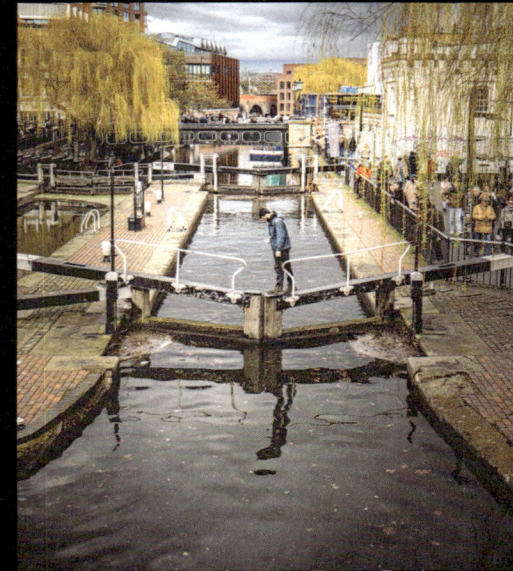
Canal Lochs, Camden Town, England

Buckingham Palace, London, England

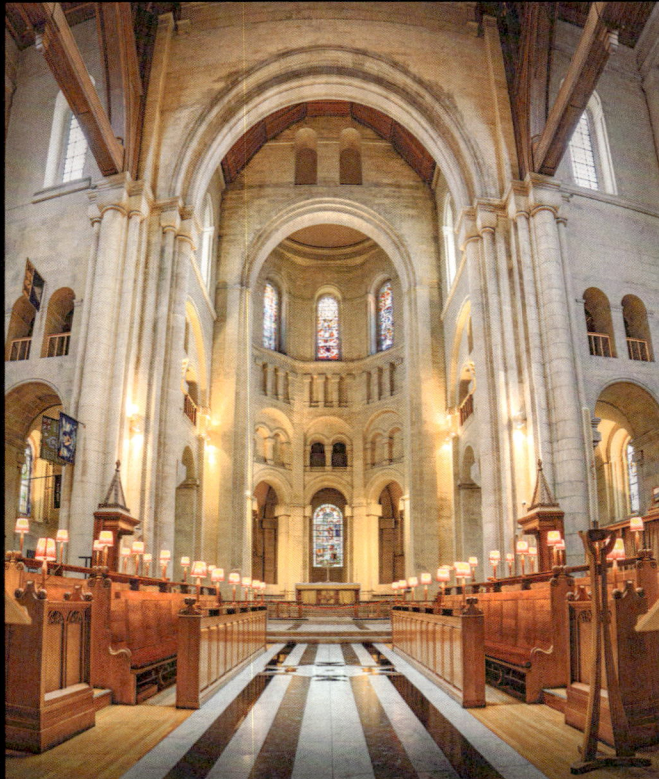
WA Art Gallery, Perth, Western Australia

St Anne's Cathedral, Belfast, Northern Ireland

London, England

www.ingramcontent.com/pod-product-compliance
Lightning Source LLC
Chambersburg PA
CBRC090735150426
42811CB00068B/1923